Our Flag Was Still There

The True Story of Mary Pickersgill
and the Star-Spangled Banner

JESSIE HARTLAND

A Paula Wiseman Book · Simon & Schuster Books for Young Readers

NEW YORK   LONDON   TORONTO   SYDNEY   NEW DELHI

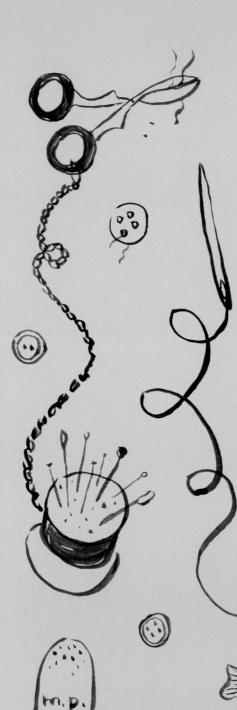

This one is for Dottie Hill Hartland,
who wrote puppet plays and designed and sewed dozens
of felt puppets for her three children

SIMON & SCHUSTER BOOKS FOR YOUNG READERS

An imprint of Simon & Schuster Children's Publishing Division

1230 Avenue of the Americas, New York, New York 10020 · Copyright © 2019 by Jessie Hartland

All rights reserved, including the right of reproduction in whole or in part in any form.

SIMON & SCHUSTER BOOKS FOR YOUNG READERS is a trademark of Simon & Schuster, Inc.

For information about special discounts for bulk purchases, please contact Simon & Schuster Special Sales at
1-866-506-1949 or business@simonandschuster.com. · The Simon & Schuster Speakers Bureau can bring authors to your
live event. For more information or to book an event, contact the Simon & Schuster Speakers Bureau at 1-866-248-3049
or visit our website at www.simonspeakers.com. · Book design by Lucy Ruth Cummins · The text for this book was set in
1689 GLC Garamond. · The illustrations for this book were rendered in gouache.

Manufactured in China · 0324 SCP · First Edition

4 6 8 10 9 7 5 3

CIP data for this book is available from the Library of Congress.

ISBN 978-1-5344-0233-1 · ISBN 978-1-5344-0234-8 (eBook)

THE YEAR WAS 1813.

Only thirty years had passed since America's thirteen colonies fought long and hard for independence from Great Britain . . . and we wanted to be free.

But in 1813 we were once again at war with England, the world's most powerful nation.

And the British were on their way to capture Baltimore, a thriving port city near the nation's capital.

The British are coming!

It was another muggy June day in Baltimore. There stood Major George Armistead, ready to lead American troops to defend Fort McHenry.

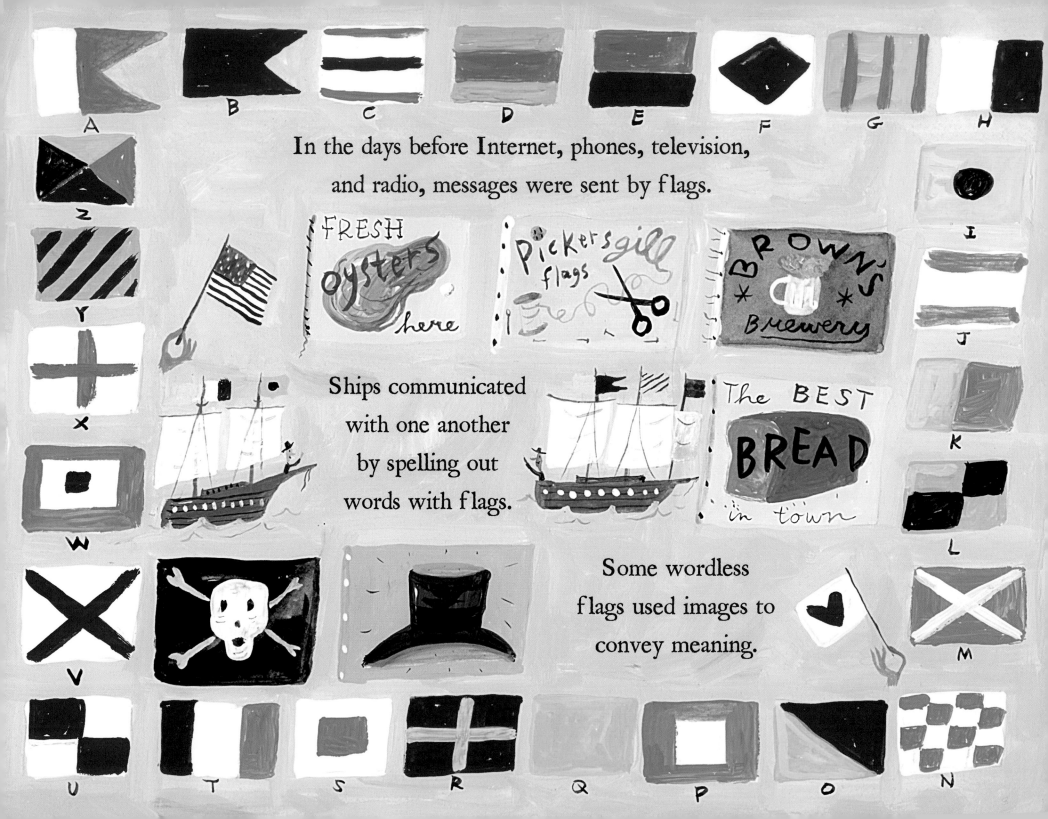

In the days before Internet, phones, television, and radio, messages were sent by flags.

Ships communicated with one another by spelling out words with flags.

Some wordless flags used images to convey meaning.

George wanted to send a big message to the British:
This land belongs to America!

But who could
make such a flag?

oysters

Lucky for George,
not far
away . . .

lived Mary Pickersgill.

Mary had learned the flag-making trade from her widowed mother,

who had also made blankets and uniforms during the **Revolutionary War.**

By now, Mary was
widowed herself.
She owned and ran
her own business,

THE BEST CRABCAKES IN BALTIMORE

and she had help from her mother, daughter,
two nieces, and an indentured servant.

Were Mary and her team up for the job?

It was a shop operated entirely by women. Back then, that was very unusual.

It's BIG and it's a rush. It's a BIG RUSH. Can you do it?

And they had just weeks to make it.
The British were on their way.

Day and night, night
and day, the women
worked together.

Each tiny stitch was a small step toward a big flag—and freedom from British rule. The flag grew and grew.

When they ran out of fabric, more was delivered, along with other supplies.

the half-finished flag . . .

was moved . . .

across the street to a brewery.

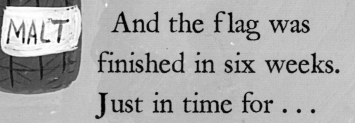

And the flag was
finished in six weeks.
Just in time for . . .

the British to retreat
to the West Indies
at summer's end.
Chilly weather was
coming.

The new flag was hoisted
over the fort anyway.

But the war waged on and America was losing.
A year went by.

In the summer of **1814**, the British attacked Washington, DC.
The capitol was in ruins, the White House was burning,
and the British were again on their way to Baltimore!
Would they attack this time?

Pow! Boom! Bam!

Under a stormy sky at Fort McHenry, sixteen British
ships attacked, firing bombs and screaming rockets.

American gunners returned the fire, shooting cannonballs and mortars.
The wind whipped, the lightning cracked, and the thunder roared.
The battle went on for twenty-five hours, and both sides were drenched.

As dawn came and the storm pulled
away, the flag peeked out of the clouds.

The British
retreated and the
battle was over!
The people of
Baltimore awoke
to see that their
enormous flag was
still there.

Meanwhile, all through the battle and the following celebration, American poet and lawyer Francis Scott Key was detained in a meeting on a British boat.

As the sun rose Key saw the huge flag still flying over the fort and was inspired to write a poem in honor of the victory.

The poem was set to a popular tune and became the lyrics to a song.

After generations, the song eventually became our national anthem.

What happened to the flag?

Well, it became the property of George Armistead's heirs.

For over one hundred years, the old flag was occasionally paraded out,

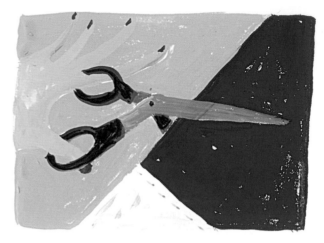

sometimes snipped at for souvenirs,

and stuffed into a safe-deposit box in New York City.

In 1912, it was given to the Smithsonian Institution in Washington, DC,

where it was restored.

Then it was crammed into a case, where it was eaten by moths.

More than fifty years later, in 1964, a new, bigger museum was built with a specially designed space for the flag.

In 1996, a design team planned a new exhibit, which included a total restoration of the flag.

Conservators carefully snipped off 1.7 million tiny stitches of the old cloth backing,

cleaned it with over ten thousand sponges, and carefully attached a new backing.

The flag, at that point over two hundred years old, had a new home in a display case that controlled the light, humidity, and temperature.

Today, if you go to the
Smithsonian's National Museum
of American History,
you can see Mary's flag.

Have you ever
seen a bigger flag?

When you sing "The Star-Spangled Banner," remember Major Armistead and his wish for America to be a free country.

Remember Francis Scott Key, who was inspired by this very same flag to write these words. Remember Mary Pickersgill and her can-do team of seamstresses.

The STAR-SPANGLED BANNER
O! Say can you see by the dawn's early light,
what so proudly we hailed
at the twilight's last gleaming,
whose broad stripes and bright stars
through the perilous fight,

AUTHOR'S NOTE

The War of 1812 was a military conflict between the United States and Great Britain over borders and international trade. It lasted three years. By the war's end, the issues had been resolved, peace was returned, and no borders were changed.

It's known that the star-spangled banner was indeed flying over Fort McHenry on the morning after the storm and battle. What is unclear is: Was it flying all night, or was it substituted for a smaller, "storm" flag in the morning? For the sake of simplification, I have only mentioned the larger flag in this book.

Mary Pickersgill was helped by her thirteen-year-old daughter, Caroline; her nieces Eliza and Margaret Young; her mother Rebecca, age 73 at the time; and an African American indentured servant, Grace Wisher. At age ten, Grace began a six-year arrangement under Mary Pickersgill, in which Mary taught Grace about housework and sewing and provided food and lodging in exchange for labor. Grace was thirteen at the time she helped sew the flag.

Who won the war? Both sides simply wore themselves out. It was after the battle of Fort McHenry that the British sought armistice. The Treaty of Ghent was signed in Belgium in December of 1814, officially ending the war.

Francis Scott Key wrote four stanzas for "The Star-Spangled Banner," but only the first one is commonly sung today. The lyrics are set to the tune of what, in the 1800s, was a popular British tavern song written by John Stafford Smith, a London-based composer.

The song gained popularity in the nineteenth century and was played at parades, concerts, and ball games. In 1931, it was officially made the national anthem. Over time, musicians have done their own versions of it, including Jimi Hendrix's famous performance at Woodstock in 1969.

Betsy Ross is often credited with the design of the American flag, although this is the source of much debate. The original American flag had thirteen stripes and thirteen stars, reflecting the original thirteen colonies that declared independence from Britain.

The flag discussed in this book was the second official version of it. It had fifteen stripes and fifteen stars, acknowledging the two newest states at that time: Kentucky and Vermont. In 1818, the United States Congress passed an act to revert to the flag's original design, with thirteen stripes to honor the original thirteen colonies, and to continue adding a star for each new state.

Major Armistead's heirs gave the flag to the Smithsonian Institution on the condition that it never be loaned out. They wanted the flag always on view for people to see when they visited Washington. The museum has kept its word with one notable exception: Fearing enemy attack during World War II, the flag was moved temporarily out of the city for safekeeping.

When the star-spangled banner was last restored, the work was done in a glassed-in lab so that the public could still see the flag and watch the restoration process. The museum's intention was to clean and preserve the old flag, not make it look fresh and new like the day it was made. Many years ago, before the flag was given to the Smithsonian, snippets were cut off as mementos and further damage was done by moths. Pages 36 and 37 accurately depict the flag's imperfections.

The building where Mary Pickersgill lived and made the flag is still there, on the corner of Albemarle and Pratt, and is now a museum. It's at 844 E. Pratt Street, Baltimore. (Visit flaghouse.org for information.)

You can also visit Fort McHenry. It's a national monument and is open year-round.

Go see the flag! It is still displayed at the Smithsonian's National Museum of American History: 1300 Constitution Avenue, NW, Washington, DC. The museum is open every day except December 25, and it is always free.

—J. H.

SOURCE NOTES

"... it is my desire to have a flag so large that the British will have no difficulty seeing it from a distance."
Taylor, Kendrick, and Brodie, *The Star-Spangled Banner*, 63.

"Our enemy is at the door!"
Ibid., 67

BIBLIOGRAPHY

Benn, Carl. *The War of 1812*. Essential Histories. Great Britain: Osprey Publishing, 2002.

Borneman, Walter R. *1812: The War that Forged a Nation*. New York: HarperCollins, 2004.

Greenblatt, Miriam. *The War of 1812*. America at War. New York: Facts on File, 1994.

O'Prey, Maureen. *Brewing in Baltimore*. "Images of America." Arcadia Publishing, 2011.

Taylor, Lonn, Kathleen M. Kendrick and Jeffrey L. Brodie. *The Star-Spangled Banner: The Making of an American Icon*. Washington, DC: Smithsonian Books, 2008.

Whitehorne, Joseph A., and Carleton Jones. *The Battle for Baltimore: 1814*. Baltimore: Nautical & Aviation Publishing Company of America, 1997.

FURTHER READING

Schultz, Randy. *Washington Ablaze: The War of 1812*. Events in American History. Rourke Pub Group, 2007.

Yuen, Helen and Asantewa Boakyewa. *The African American Girl Who Helped Make the Star-Spangled Banner*. http://americanhistory.si.edu. The National Museum of American History. May 2014.

TIMELINE

Early 1800s: War rages between England and France over trade.

1807: Trying to stay out of the conflict, America enacts the unpopular Embargo Act, ending trade with Europe. No more trade with Europe cripples American businesses.

June 18, 1812: The US declares war on Britain.

1813, summer: George Armistead, Commander of Baltimore's Fort McHenry, commissions two flags from Mary Pickersgill.

August 24, 1814: The British burn down the White House and other buildings in Washington, DC, and head for Baltimore.

September 12-14, 1814: The United States defends Baltimore's Fort McHenry. The British retreat, and Mary Pickersgill's flag is raised.

December 24, 1814: Both sides sign the Treaty of Ghent. The flag becomes property of Major Armistead's family.

February 1815: The treaty is ratified by the US, ending the war and returning the countries to prewar status quo.

July 5, 1907: The flag, now the property of Eben Appleton, George Armistead's grandson, is lent to the Smithsonian Museum and travels there by overnight train.

1912: The loan is converted to a gift, and the flag is restored by the Smithsonian.

March 3, 1931: "The Star-Spangled Banner" is made the national anthem by congressional resolution, which is signed by President Herbert Hoover.